Leade

Beginning:

Training for More

Joshua David Mickley

Promised Land Leadership Press, LLC

Forward: Dr. Ralph Mickley, PhD

Leadership in the Beginning: Training for More
Genesis 1:1 – 16:15

1st Edition, 1st Printing, May 2026

Cataloging-in-Publication data on file with the Library of Congress

Mickley, Joshua David
Leadership in the Beginning: Training for More
Claremore, OK: Promised Land Leadership Press, LLC

ISBN 979-8-9957872-0-4

Printed in the United States of America

Table of Contents

Foreword

How to Use This Book 1

Part I: Training for More (Genesis 1:1 – 16:15)

Let's Begin Here: Preparation for Heaven 5

Chapter 1: He Rested 13

Chapter 2: Delegate & Entrust 21

Chapter 3: Taking Responsibility 27

Chapter 4: Justice & Compassion..................33

Chapter 5: Brother's Keeper 41

Chapter 6: Obedience to God 49

Chapter 7: Persistence & Patience 57

Chapter 8: Communication 65

Chapter 9: Trusting God 73

Chapter 10: Honesty 81

Chapter 11: Peacemaker 87

Chapter 12: Surrounded 95

Chapter 13: Waiting 103

Putting It All Together 111

Bibliography 119

Acknowledgements

I would first like to thank my Lord and Savior, Jesus Christ, for blessing me with the ability, motivation, and opportunity to write this book. Without His guidance and provision, none of this would have been possible. I am also deeply grateful to the Holy Spirit for the constant inspiration, direction, and words that have shaped these pages. It is my prayer that these words will reach leaders at every level and inspire them to create stronger, healthier environments for those they lead.

To my parents, thank you for your unwavering support, encouragement, and the foundation you built in my life. Your influence has shaped who I am today, and I am forever grateful.

To my wife, Janine, thank you for your patience, love, and constant support throughout this journey. Your belief in me has been a steady source of strength. To my daughter and son-in-law, thank you for your encouragement and for always standing beside me as I pursued this calling.

I would also like to extend my sincere thanks to Pastor Aaron, Recovery Pastor at Cedar Point Church in Claremore, Oklahoma. Your willingness to share your time, talent, and creativity in developing the cover for this book is deeply appreciated.

To each of you, thank you for being part of this journey.

Forward

The book you are about to read is about "Leadership". It is not your ordinary or typical book rehashing the same old material just written by a different author.

I believe you will find this book refreshing, thought provoking, enlightening, challenging and enjoyable.

You may find that your "Leadership position" has a purpose bigger than you ever thought or dreamed.

Each chapter is purposely written with you in mind. They are short for a reason; to give you an opportunity to reflect on what you just read and allow you time to answer several questions rather than just load you down with information.

No matter what "Leadership position" you hold or you are pursuing, this book is for you. Yes, CEO, Vice President, Manager, Supervisor or employee, this book will give you important information and common-sense insight to empower you to do your job better.

Pick up a copy for your entire staff and associates. Raise the standards of your company and help everyone become the best they can be. Build a company that will serve your clients and help make you proud of the business you provide to your community.

Now I'm proud to introduce you to the author of this book, my son, Joshua Mickley.

-Ralph Mickley, Ph.D. in Marriage/Family Counseling and Th.D. – retired Pastor (50 years) – Leading and Discipling people.

How to Use This Book

This book is the first in a four-part series that explores what the book of Genesis teaches us about leadership. In the author's view, effective leadership is increasingly absent in our society today. This lack of leadership can be seen at every level—from the nation's capital in Washington, D.C., through state governments, businesses, through our corporations, and ultimately into our schools and homes.

In the environment we find ourselves in today, future generations have little opportunity to learn and develop strong leadership because true leadership is rarely modeled for them. Without visible examples of integrity, responsibility, and service, it becomes increasingly difficult for the next generation to understand what genuine leadership looks like.

Fortunately, there is a place we can turn to reset and rediscover what effective leadership truly means. While Jesus Christ stands as the ultimate example of leadership—demonstrating servant leadership during His time on Earth—the entire Bible contains lessons that guide us toward our true responsibilities as leaders. Scripture provides timeless principles that can help restore and strengthen leadership in every area of life.

This book and series was designed especially for Small Groups, Life Groups, and Home Groups. Each chapter is intended to be studied over the course of a week, allowing groups to read, reflect, ask questions, and discuss the themes presented. The books in this series are organized into semester-length sections to align with the schedules of many church groups. This structure allows for natural breaks during the year and provides flexibility to study other topics as well. Leadership is an important subject, but maintaining balance helps ensure that groups remain engaged and avoid burnout.

At the same time, this book is also a valuable resource for individuals who wish to develop their leadership abilities independently. The author recommends approaching the book one chapter per week. Spend time each day reflecting on the chapter's theme, reviewing the Scripture passages referenced, and thoughtfully responding to the reflection questions provided at the end of each chapter. There is no need to rush through the material. Allow yourself time to absorb the lessons and to listen for God's guidance as He shapes and directs your leadership journey.

This book may also serve as a helpful resource for pastors seeking ideas and inspiration for sermons. While respecting all applicable copyright guidelines, pastors are encouraged to draw from the concepts presented here as they guide their congregations toward stronger, more faithful leadership.

It is important to remember that leadership begins in the home and extends outward into every part of society. For that reason, the principles discussed in this book are not limited to traditional leadership roles such as politicians, executives, or managers. They are equally relevant for teachers, coaches, parents, and anyone who influences the lives of others.

It is my hope that you will find this book both enjoyable and beneficial in your current leadership journey. When you complete this volume, be sure to continue exploring the remaining books in the series, as they are released, as we further examine the leadership lessons found throughout Scripture.

Let's Begin Here:

Preparation for Heaven

"I knew you before I formed you in your mother's womb. Before you were born I set you apart and appointed you as my prophet to the nations." (Jeremiah 1:5, NLT)

This lesson will, if nothing else, give us something to think about, as we take a deeper look at just what God has planned for us. Think for a moment about a God who not only pre-existed time, but who created time. A God who created this world and knew every action that every creature would make before a living being ever existed on this Earth. A God who knew us before He had even formed us in our mothers' wombs. This same God has called us to be leaders and to represent Him to a specific group of individuals who He wants to show His goodness and love to. But why would we limit His plans for us?

Philippians 3:20 informs us, “But we are citizens of Heaven, where the Lord Jesus Christ lives. And we are eagerly waiting for him to return as our Savior” (NLT). If our citizenship is in Heaven, and we are only visitors passing through here, why would we limit God’s plans for us to this time and this Earth? Isn’t it likely that what God has designed and appointed for us here in this life is preparation for what He has planned for us in Eternity? Let’s entertain this idea a little further with an open mind.

God has designed us to fulfill His will that He has designed us for, and as leaders this includes serving people and directing them towards Jesus so that they can then accomplish the goals that God has created them to undertake. Additionally, Colossians 3:23 tells us that everything we do is to be done as though we are doing it for God, and not for other men (NLT). We are called to be the best that we can be in all that we do; and might this be because God wants us putting all of our effort into the training that He has called us to in preparation for Eternity?

This is preceded by Colossians 3:1-2 that reminds us that since we have been risen with Christ that we should be striving for Heavenly goals because that is where we find Jesus; and this verse reiterates that things of Heaven are much more important than things here on Earth

(NLT). Our day-to-day lives, while they are important to us, are not what we need to be concentrating on. Instead, in everything we do, we need to be thinking about Heaven and the impacts each of our decisions today will have on us, and others, in Eternity. As leaders, we should see our roles as training for possible activities we will take part in once we leave this Earth and attain our Heavenly roles.

Why do we limit God's plans for us? Is it possible that God has plans for us far beyond our lives here on Earth? 1 Corinthians 2:9 informs us that we as humans cannot even begin to comprehend through sight, hearing, or imagination, just what God has in store for us (NLT). God lives outside of our defined space and time. He has created all of us for a specific reason and purpose; and what could possibly limit His plans for us to this time and space? The answer is, nothing.

We have no idea of all the intricacies that we will find in Heaven, including different roles that we might fill there. Is there a possibility that God will have a need for leaders in Heaven? Well, we just read that we cannot even fathom what He has prepared for us, so the possibility exists that we may be in training here on Earth for holy and spirituals roles that God may have prepared and is holding for us in Eternity, including leadership roles. This should change our outlook on how we see our roles as leaders here in this life.

Regardless of whether or not this idea becomes reality, we are called to perform our best and represent God in all we do. Heaven is our end-goal, so we need to continually keep our eyes on that prize. As we continue to fulfill the callings that God has created us to satisfy, we will hopefully be impacting individuals we lead and others around us for God. Our ultimate reward will be seeing people that we have impacted once we get to Heaven.

However, God has promised to bless us for following His will and walking in concert with Him. Some of those blessings will be here on Earth, but many of our blessings will be in Heaven. 1 Peter 1:4 speaks to us of an inheritance for each of us that is uncontaminated and unblemished, and that cannot be altered or corroded (NLT). Our rewards are kept for us in Heaven. This lesson is just tossing out the idea that some of our rewards might turn out to be various roles that are waiting for those of us who strive to successfully accomplish and learn from the responsibilities given to us here in this life.

As you move through the remainder of this book, consider how each topic might be an opportunity to improve yourself for eternal responsibilities. Take the time to imagine what God might have in store for you once you reach Heaven. Spend a moment during each study to thank God for caring about you enough to have planned your life and eternity from the beginning of time. Then, make a conscious effort every day to become a better leader that God can use here on Earth as well as in Eternity.

Study Prayer

Heavenly Father, thank You for creating me, and for having a plan for my life before I was even born. I ask You to allow me to use the things from this book to become a better leader for my team, for my organization, and for You. Please allow me to consider with an open mind what I might be learning here, for my assignment in Eternity. Amen.

Questions

- Do You believe that God could be preparing individuals for "Eternal Roles" that He has creates us for? Explain.

- If our citizenship is in Heaven, why would God limit our calling to this earth and this time?

- Explain how doing everything for the Lord here on earth can prepare us for roles that might be waiting for us in Heaven.

- Explain why you believe the Bible continually tells us to keep our minds turned towards Heavenly things and not earthly things.

- Just dreaming about Heaven, discuss what you believe things will be like in Heaven. Will Heaven be a continual worship service? Do you see angels playing harps on clouds? Might we possibly have responsibilities and duties to perform?

- Does the possibility of God having an "Eternal Leadership Role" for you in Heaven change your outlook on the way you perform your leadership role now? If so, how? If not, why?

He Rested

"On the seventh day God had finished his work of creation, so he rested from all his work. And God blessed the seventh day and declared it holy because it was a day when he rested from all his work of creation." (Genesis 2:2-3, NLT)

In the beginning…the first chapter of Genesis lays out just how God went about creating the Earth, all that the Earth contains, along with all the expanses that man has been striving to learn about and explore since they were created. In addition to telling us exactly how everything we know came into being, God shows us by example what he expects from us as leaders by working hard, completing the job, then taking time to rest. He took six days to complete all his work, then rested on the seventh day. This was so important to God that he blessed and sanctified the seventh day.

This importance carried on into the Laws handed down to the Israelites in Exodus 20:8 when God commanded the people to "remember to observe the Sabbath Day by keeping it holy" (NLT). The significance of rest and the Sabbath was again stressed in Exodus 35:2-3 when Moses reported to the Israelites what God had commanded of them telling them that six days of the week were designed for work, but the seventh day was set aside as a day of rest and reflection to God; and that even so much as the lighting of a fire would result in death (NLT).

God valued this day of rest so much that he mandated such menial tasks such as lighting a fire to warm your house as wrong, or more likely because lighting that fire might lead to further work such as cooking. The important lesson is that God treasured rest so much that he ordered that anyone who did any work on the Sabbath should be put to death.

So, the question becomes, why was a day of rest so important to God; and the answer to this is for several reasons. First, He had worked for 6 days creating the beautiful world in which we live and all it contains, and He wanted us to enjoy His creation while acknowledging His work. This makes it seem as though the seventh day, the day of rest, the Sabbath, was strictly a religious command. A command about honoring God for the work he had done to complete the creation we live in, but this fails to take into account other important reasons God has mandated this downtime.

For instance, secondly, God, knowing everything, saw that He would be creating a companion for man, and that relationship would lead to families, and friends, and that these groups would require some of our time in order to retain a healthy bond and connection. Or third, being our Creator, God knew that humans would require time off, rest, downtime in order to remain healthy. God was looking ahead at His creation and laying out the foundations for its success going into the future.

Jesus reiterated this point in Mark 2:27 when confronted by Pharisees who were chastising He and His disciples for breaking the Sabbath Law. (Let's remember that the religious leaders at the time had added their own twists to God's laws in an attempt to control the people and stand superior to them.) Jesus rebuked these Pharisees and told them that "the Sabbath was made to meet the needs of people, and not people to meet the requirements of the Sabbath" (NLT).

As most things said by Jesus, this had many meanings, but the overlaying meaning was that God created the Sabbath because He knew man would need rest. This relates to us as leaders in several capacities. To begin with, we need to understand the importance of time off for those we lead; but just as important, we need to understand how critical time off is for us and those we love.

How egotistical of us to read how God took a day of rest and not see that we as humans need rest even more. Let's all learn from God's first lesson to leaders and begin to value downtime as much as God does.

Study Prayer

Heavenly Father, thank You for this beautiful world that You created for me. Thank You for setting the example for me of completing my work, then taking time to rest and recoup with my family and friends. Dear God, thank You for my family and friends. Thank You for knowing Your creation well enough to understand how critical rest is to health. Moving forward, dear God, please remind me the importance of rest for myself as well as for those I lead. Help me to understand how this will be important in Eternity as well. In Your Name I pray, Amen.

Questions

- Do you take time off from work weekly? How do you spend this time?

- As a leader, do you honor time off for those you lead, and express how important this time is to regenerate so they can be healthier personally and better prepared to be a successful member of your team?

- Explain what the word “sanctified” means.

- What other reasons do you believe God might have for valuing time off for mankind?

- Explain how Exodus 35 shows us just how important the day of rest was/is to God. Discuss why death is no longer an issue for those who do not observe the Sabbath.

- Explain additional reasons for Jesus' statement in Mark 2:27 where he said that “the Sabbath was made for man, not man for the Sabbath.”

Reflection

Take a moment to reflect on this study and how putting this topic into practice can help prepare you for Eternity.

Delegate & Entrust

"So the Lord God formed from the ground all the wild animals and all the birds of the sky. He brought them to the man to see what he would call them, and the man chose the name for each one."
(Genesis 2:19, NLT)

God created the galaxies, universe, and the Earth in the previous chapter, which included creating man in His own image. Now this chapter speaks about how God formed the animals of the fields and birds of the air to fill the Earth. If He was able to create everything we see and know, then He easily could have named the creatures He was placing in His creation. Instead, He brought the land animals and creatures of the air before the man and trusted him to give them names. He did not micromanage the process, but allowed the man to do the job he had been given.

Delegating & Entrusting is a theme discussed early in the Bible. Exodus 18:13-27 tells the story of Moses sitting as Judge over the Israelites, hearing and deciding everyday cases that were brought before him. His father-in-law, seeing the amount of work being handed over to Moses, advised him to select other men, train them, and then allow them to judge the lower cases. This would leave Moses to judge only the larger cases that could not be decided by the other men. This took pressure off of Moses and allowed him to concentrate on other areas where he was needed as the leader of the Israelites (NLT).

The Bible encourages delegation. Once we have selected individuals or teams to perform a function, and once we have delegated work, allowing them to complete their task(s) without micromanaging reaffirms and inspires our teams while expressing confidence in ourselves. Additionally, this shows respect for these individuals, as well as to God who created them in His image.

Psalms 139:13-14 expresses poetically how we are creations of God who formed us in our mother's wombs. This passage states, "You make all the delicate, inner parts of my body and knit me together in my mother's womb.

Thank You for making me so wonderfully complex! Your workmanship is marvelous—how well I know it" (NLT).

We as leaders are tasked with guiding and coaching those we lead. A coach doesn't play the game for the players, and we shouldn't be in the middle of tasks we have handed over to others to complete. Instead, we need to allow these individuals or teams to complete their work while making ourselves available to advise when needed. We need to allow the blessings who God has placed on our teams to use the gifts that He has placed within them, and by doing this we show respect to God by respecting those He created.

Study Prayer

Dear God, thank You for modelling the act of delegating and entrusting to me. Please allow me to see the value of each individual that You have placed on my team. Help me to honor you by honoring their skills and allowing them to complete their work. Please show me when to step in and to what level to be involved in order to help each team member. Thank You for guiding me away from being a micro-manager. Amen.

Questions

- Do you struggle with delegating and entrusting?

- What dichotomy do you see with delegating and entrusting?

- Is there ever a legitimate place for micro-managing?

- How does micro-managing disrespect those you lead? How does it disrespect God?

- In Exodus 18:13-27, what is the main purpose for delegating and entrusting?

- Explain how our existence represents God.

- Does our treatment of each other truly reflect our respect for God? How? Why?

Reflection

Take a moment to reflect on this study and how putting this topic into practice can help prepare you for Eternity.

Taking Responsibility

"The man replied, 'It was the woman you gave me who gave me the fruit, and I ate it.'" (Genesis 3:12, NLT)

In the early chapters of Genesis, we learned that God had created the perfect garden, Eden, and had placed Adam and Eve within it to live there and care for the garden. In that perfect garden man and woman had a relationship with God that included taking walks with Him in the coolness of the evenings. God gave the man and woman dominion over everything in the garden and allowed them to eat of the fruit from all of the trees of the garden except for the tree in the center of the garden, the Tree of Knowledge of Good and Evil.

Being imperfect humans, they allowed the temptation from the serpent to take hold and Eve ate of the forbidden tree, she then turned and offered the fruit to Adam. Immediately, sin entered the world and they both knew that they had done wrong. This leads us to the point of this study which is Adam's failure of leadership. When God approached Adam and Eve and questioned them, instead of taking responsibility, Adam blamed his wife for their actions.

Due to the actions taken by the man and woman, an entire slew of scourges were laid out in Genesis 3:14-19. Galatians 6:7 tells us that we are only fooling ourselves if we do not realize that our actions have unintended consequences (NLT). So going back to our story in Eden, sin entered the world by the actions of the man and woman which resulted in the curses laid out by God; and now we can wonder if any of these afflictions would have differed if Adam had just taken responsibility for their actions, instead of trying to pass blame.

When God gives us liabilities and responsibilities, He expects us to manage these situations in a way that honors Him. This includes taking responsibility of how we lead and actions both we and our teams take.
2 Corinthians 9:6 informs us that when we put in little effort, the results will be little; however, when we put in great effort, the results will be great (NLT).

The results of putting in great effort might entail receiving more responsibilities, or maybe gaining dedication and respect from those we lead for our willingness to "sow bountifully." And I'm sure we can all think of negatives we might receive for sowing sparingly. Harry Truman had a sign on his Oval Office desk that read, "The Buck Stops Here." We should lead the same way, by taking responsibility for the good and the bad that happens under our purview.

Study Prayer

Dear Heavenly Father. Thank You for entrusting me with leading these individuals that You care so much about. I ask You to enable me to be faithful to them individually and as a whole, even when times are tough. Holy Spirit, I pray that You will give me the strength and the courage to step up and take responsibility even when I may feel like the outcome was not my fault. Allow me to represent You to each person I lead through my ability to take accountability for the team, while relinquishing glory to them when things go well. I ask You this in Your Holy Name, Amen.

Questions

- Do you find it hard to take responsibility for bad outcomes that result under your leadership?

- Explain a time when you have stepped in and taken responsibility for a subordinate's actions (Buck Stops Here). Explain the circumstances.

- Explain what "whatever a man sows this he will reap" means to you.

- Give some examples of how sowing sparingly or bountifully has played out in your life.

- Discuss some reaping that may occur for a leader who “sows sparingly.”

- Explain how a leader can model responsibility to those they lead. Explain what type of responsibility leaders can expect from those they lead.

Reflection

Take a moment to reflect on this study and how putting this topic into practice can help prepare you for Eternity.

Dismiss From Mind (Justice/Compassion)

"And the Lord God made clothing from animal skins for Adam and his wife." (Genesis 3:21, NLT)

Now Adam and Eve had both sinned against God. Not only had they sinned but they had tried to hide themselves, some would say in shame; although, if really looked at, wasn't it really about avoiding consequences? Much like modern day organizations establish a leadership structure, God had established Adam as the head; yet as we learned in the last lesson, he tried to "Pass the Buck" on to his wife and blame her for their sin, and ultimately God for creating her.

God was furious with the man and woman's disobedience, laying out punishments to the serpent, the woman, and the man. Each individual's punishment was unique to them. Then at the end of Genesis 3, Adam and Eve were both driven out of the garden because God is just and follows through with His words.

However, Genesis 3:21 shows us how God's love and compassion remains for us regardless of the trouble we find ourselves facing. In the midst of his punishment, God took the time to meet the needs of the sinners right there where they were. He made garments for the two of them so that they could hide their nakedness and shame. God showed us how He expects us to act as leaders. He expects us to treat those that He entrusts in our care with compassion and justice.

Leviticus 26:14-46 lays out a list of consequences for disobedience, but circles back to redemption once amends had been made (NLT). God is not a one and done kind of God, and he expects us to lead as He does when dealing with his people (those HE has placed under our care). This does not mean that disciplining is never and option, it just means that dealing with people where they are is more important.

It is important to lead people with compassion and with the ability for people to regain favor. Psalms 103:12 says, "He has removed our sins as far from us as the east is from the west" (NLT). Now we are not God. We tend to operate with a "forgive but not forget" type mentality. That is important these days, as documentation is critical in today's legalistic world; but at the same time, employees' past actions should not be held against them outside of context nor on a day-to-day basis. Meaning, only bring up past actions for reoccurrences.

In concluding this study, God has modeled His desired leadership for His creation, and we should strive to honor God by acting the same way towards the people He places under our care.

Study Prayer

Heavenly Father. Along with my previous prayer asking for the ability to take responsibility, I also ask You for Your compassion. Give me judgement on when I should proceed with some sort of justice, and let me know just how far that should extend. Give me an abundance of empathy, as I would request the same of You towards myself. Thank You for Your wisdom in each circumstance, and allow those I lead to see my decision as compassion and not weakness. Thank You in advance for allowing me to set an example of You to my team. In Your Name I pray, Amen.

Questions

- Explain the meaning behind the animal that was used to provide the skin that God used to clothe Adam and Eve.

- Do you tend to hold perceived past transgressions against those under your leadership, or do you allow them to move past their mistakes? Explain.

- Explain what instances you believe warrant moving past progressive discipline and compassion and straight to suspension or termination.

- Discuss a time, in your leadership role, where you have shown compassion in the midst of a circumstance that would typically result in discipline.

- Explain how in today's world compassion and discipline can work together.

- Discuss how, in your life, God has shown you compassion in the midst of a time of discipline.

Reflection

Take a moment to reflect on this study and how putting this topic into practice can help prepare you for Eternity.

Brother's Keeper

"Afterward the Lord asked Cain, 'Where is your brother? Where is Abel?' 'I don't know,' Cain responded. 'Am I my brother's guardian?'" (Genesis 4:9, NLT)

As leaders, we understand that short of a self-defense type situation, we will never lay a hand on anyone we lead. With that being said, in Genesis 4 we learn about Cain and Abel; and through this we see that out of an act of jealousy, Cain had murdered his brother Abel and disposed of his body. When questioned about the whereabouts of Abel, Cain replied by asking, "am I my brother's guardian (or keeper)?" Not only was Cain responsible for Abel's demise, but as the older brother, Cain was viewed by God as a leader and a caretaker of his younger brother. This brings us to the topic of today's discussion.

Understanding that God places us where he can use us most effectively, being in a leadership position means that He needs us to care for others, namely those he has entrusted under our care as leaders. He expects us to fulfill this role by being their (our brother/sister's) keeper. In honoring God in this role, He expects us to love those He has placed under our purview. This means dealing with them by showing empathy, understanding, and respect, while having their backs.

Proverbs 17:17 states, "A friend is always loyal, and a brother is born to help in times of need" (NLT). God expects us to treat those we lead as a friend and as a brother. This means being there for them both in work situations and whatever personal issues they may open up to us about. We are actually God's representatives to them.

Remember the story from Mark 12:28-31 where a Scribe questioned Jesus asking what commandment was the greatest. Jesus replied that we are to love God with all of our heart, soul, mind, and strength; but then He followed this up by saying we **SHALL** (not may, not should, not could) but shall love your neighbor as yourself (NLT). We actually show God love by showing love to those He places under our leadership.

Jesus reiterates the importance of loving each other to His disciples in John 15:12-14 when He commands them to love one another as He had loved them. He went as far as to say that true love is being willing to give up your life for another (NLT), then He proceeded to model this for us all.

God places specific people in our lives and under our leadership in order for us to model His love to them. So, are we "our brother's keeper?" Absolutely! While we live our lives, God lives in His reality. While we live thinking we are just working a job, God's sole purpose is for us to reach others for Him.

Study Prayer

Lord Jesus. You have given me a responsibility to watch over, care for, and lead a group of individuals who are special to You. Please give me the peace, patience, and understanding to not only meet these requirements, but in the process to represent You well. Holy Spirit, be with me in all I do, and help my actions to always show that I am my brother's keeper. Thank You in advance for making me the leader that You designed me to be. In Your Holy Name, Amen.

Questions

- Explain what "being your brother's keeper" means to you.

- Do you believe your leadership role(s) are more than just a job or an aspect of your life? Explain.

- What does the word "**SHALL**" mean to you? Does any aspect of your job distinguish between shall, should, and could?

- Do you have individuals under your leadership who are difficult to love? How do you address this issue?

- What can you do regularly, going forward, to model God's love for those you lead? What specifically can you do to show love to those you find difficult to love?

Reflection

Take a moment to reflect on this study and how putting this topic into practice can help prepare you for Eternity.

Obedience to God

"Build a large boat from cypress wood and waterproof it with tar, inside and out. Then construct decks and stalls throughout the interior." (Genesis 6:14, NLT)

In Genesis 6:22 we learn that, "Noah did everything exactly as God had commanded him" (NLT). In fact, Noah took decades to build the ark. People must have thought he was crazy, human-kind's first conspiracy theorist; but Noah didn't care about what anybody else thought. In his 500's, Noah listened to the command of God and built humanity's saving vessel to the exact specifications laid out by God. When the rain began to fall, and definitely 40 days later, Noah had to be ecstatic that he had obeyed God. Because Noah obeyed God, mankind continued to exist and flourish, and we are here today to study his obedience.

We learned in the previous study that as humans we often revolve our jobs and our positions around our lives and survival, and while God does provide for us through these means, His purpose(s) are much larger and revolve around drawing people to Him. While most of us will never hear God speak to us through an audible voice, He does speak to us in different ways, and it is critical that we are listening to and obedient to what He is telling us. Directions God gives us might not save humanity, but may be critical in keeping us out of trouble, and most certainly will be critical for the success of our groups and those we lead.

In essence, listening to God opens the door and allows us to be our "brother's keeper." Exodus 19:5 tells us that if we obey God and keep His covenant, that we become His special treasure set apart from other people on the earth that He created and who belongs to Him (NLT). God was explaining to Moses what the people of Israel needed to do in order to be His people. We see over and over in the Old Testament that when Israel listened to God, they prospered, but when they disobeyed, they faced destruction. This is not to say that doing your own thing as a leader will result in your group being led off to Babylon; however, God's hand will always be with those who listen to and obey Him, and will allow for His perfect plan will play out.

After wandering around in the wilderness for 40 years, Moses died and Joshua took over as leader of the people of Israel. Joshua 6:2 says, "But the Lord said to Joshua, 'I have given you Jericho, its king, and all its strong warriors" (NLT). Then God gave Joshua specific instructions explaining what the people of Israel were to do in order to defeat Jericho. The directions given were detailed and made absolutely no sense. The directions had nothing to do with battle and everything to do with focusing on God. The Israelites followed God's directions and victory was won. We must act, as leaders, in the same way. We must focus on God and listen to His quiet whispers guiding us on how we should lead and what he wants us to do. We must remember that as we live our lives, He is performing a bigger purpose through us.

Study Prayer

Dear God, I know Your ways are perfect, and I always want to be working within Your will. Please humble me to the point where every move I make is based on what You want from me. Allow my leadership to represent You well while fulfilling, through me, Your ultimate and perfect outcome. Please enable my obedience to You to impact those I lead while drawing them towards You. Thank You for making me a leader. In Jesus' Name, Amen.

Questions

- If a voice spoke to you from the ethers and directed you to build an ark because a flood was coming that would wipe out mankind, what thoughts would go through your mind?

- Read Joshua 6 & 7 and explain why Israel's battle against Jericho was overwhelming, and why the next battle against the much lesser opponent of Ai was much more devastating.

- How and when does God speak to you?

- Explain a time when you have taken time to stop, pray, and consult God about issues that you were facing in your leadership roles. How did he respond to you?

- Explain how decisions you make, and being obedient to God in your leadership role can play out as a "brother's keeper" opportunity.

- Do you have any issues you are facing that might require directions from God?

Reflection

Take a moment to reflect on this study and how putting this topic into practice can help prepare you for Eternity.

Sent It Again

Persistence & Patients

"He waited another seven days and then released the dove again. This time it did not come back." (Genesis 8:12, NLT)

As leaders we want persistence from those we lead because we understand that failure comes when we stop trying. While some individuals may have an inner drive that keeps them striving to attain their goals, most will require constant encouragement to remain persistent; and all will need to see us, their leaders, model persistence because if we're not fighting for the goal, then why should they?

Noah modeled persistence following the flood when he first sent out a raven, then over the course of the next 3 weeks sent out a dove until it finally didn't return to the ark. It was then that Noah knew that the flood waters were receding and the ground was drying up. This showed not only persistence, but patience. Just imagine being cooped up in an ark with hungry and rambunctious animals and all the smells that come along with them. However, persistence and patience are two actions that work together for success. Being persistent means that the objective we are aiming for is taking time to achieve, and the best way to successfully obtain that objective is through persistence and patience. Both are actions that leaders need to model for those they lead.

Proverbs 24:16 assures us that the righteous will stumble, but that they continue to rise, then goes on to assure that the wicked are damaged with just one blunder (NLT). This verse points out the importance of persistence in times of struggles. It promotes the need to get back up and press on when you fall. This is critical in our work lives, but as servant leaders, we strive to reach people on a personal level. If we model persistence to others, they can take these skills and implement them in their personal lives, which could impact their home lives, families, and friends. We need to allow God to use our actions as leaders to touch the lives of the people we lead in areas we could never stir on our own.

Galatians 6:9 encourages us to stay "in the fight" by informing us that we should not tire of doing what is right because if we persevere in our actions then we will reap our blessings when the time is right (NLT). The far-reaching skill of persistence holds the promise of this verse if we don't give up.

A key aspect of the promise that we need to keep in mind is that we have to be doing good. Meaning, we need to be acting in God's will, or as we learned in the previous study, listening to God, then following through with what He has told us to do. This means that success may not always look the way we want it too, but the results will be perfect. In the end, if the persistence we model to others leads them to benefit through persistence in their own personal lives, then success was achieved.

Study Prayer

Jesus, patience is a virtue that is taught throughout the Bible. Patience is important both in my personal life (waiting for You to act on my behalf) as well as in my leadership life (in my actions towards those I lead). Please teach me patience in both regards, and allow my actions concerning patience to reflect Your patience and love towards those I lead. Thank

You for helping me with my patience. In Your Name, Amen.

Questions

- Explain what persistence means to you.

- Explain how persistence and patience work together.

- How can persistence benefit us or others in our personal lives?

- How can persistence be modeled to others?

- Explain a time in your life when persistence paid off.

- Explain a time in your life when a situation did not turn out the way you had hoped. In the end, did it turn out as a success?

Reflection

Take a moment to reflect on this study and how putting this topic into practice can help prepare you for Eternity.

Communication

"Come, let's go down and confuse the people with different languages. Then they won't be able to understand each other." (Genesis 11:7, NLT)

In Genesis 11 we read the account of the Tower of Babel, and through this story we learn just how important communication is to success. Quickly, this story recounts a time when the entire world spoke one language and came together to build a city with a tower so high that it would reach the Heavens. They were doing this to make a name for themselves. In order to stop these people from being successful, God caused the people to speak various different languages, which made it impossible for them to work together to complete their project. Through this act, God showed us that as leaders, clear communication is critical to success.

As leaders it is important for us to view communication from several different angles. First of all, listening is a critical part of communication. We must listen and hear what is being said before speaking. We should not be thinking about our response while listening, and just as important is realizing that an immediate answer is not always necessary. Often times we are best served by taking what is being said under advisement, and then considering our response rather than just rushing to make a comeback. What is important here is making sure we make a point to give a response within an appropriate timeframe.

Secondly, as leaders we need to speak clearly and concisely, making sure that those we lead undoubtedly understand their expectations, and we need to expect the same type of clear and concise communication amongst our team members.

Next, and this seems obvious, as leaders we need to ensure that our team members and the various teams that we work with "speak the same language." This is important on a generational basis, but also, depending on industries. This includes defining terms and jargon used by different groups.

Lastly, as leaders we must always understand and express to others the importance that written messages (text, email, etc.) do not include tone or body language, so we need to limit immediate reactions and responses. Through all of these communicative actions we would be wise to keep in mind Proverbs 25:11 which says, "Timely advice is lovely, like golden apples in a silver basket" (NLT). We should always strive to communicate in a way that is sweet to the spirit of those we lead.

Remembering that we are placed in leadership roles by God to impact others for Him, we need to communicate in a way that is uplifting to God. This includes tone, body language, word choice, clarity, topic, and everything involving communication. A great way to start each day would be a short little prayer from Psalm 141:3, "Take control of what I say, O Lord, and guard my lips" (NLT). God understands the importance of communication, and He is longing to help guide us.

Study Prayer

Dear God, communication is so very important to living with others, but as a leader, communication is doubly important to interpersonal skills and success. I ask You right now, Holy Spirit, to guide me in my communications with everybody that I come across and especially with those that I lead. Let all my communications glorify You and point others towards You. Thank You for allowing me to communicate better with others. In Jesus' Name, Amen.

Questions

- Explain the importance of listening in communications.

- How are your listening skills? What tools can you use to practice and improve your listening skills?

- Explain in your line of work, and with those you lead, how communication is critical to success.

- Explain how generational differences can hamper communication. Explain how different groups you work with affect clear communication.

- Explain how text messages and emails can cause problems between people.

- How can our communications direct people towards God? How can it turn people from God?

Reflection

Take a moment to reflect on this study and how putting this topic into practice can help prepare you for Eternity.

Trusting God

He Will Lead You

"The Lord said to Abram, 'Leave your native country, your relatives, and your father's family, and go to the land that I will show you.'" (Genesis 12:1, NLT)

Abram was a man of faith that God had chosen to use as a starting point to begin the nation of Israel and more importantly, the lineage of Jesus; thus, creating the entry point for the Savior of the world. The first step in God's plan relied on Abram to put his complete trust in God and follow His command to leave his country, family, and everything he knew, and travel to a foreign land that he was unfamiliar with, and was not even privy to where his end-point would be. Imagine where the world would be right now if Abram had not listened and acted.

This story actually shows us the actions of two different leaders. God showed us the leadership example of picking the right person for the job, then sitting back and allowing him to make the right decisions. Abram, on the other hand showed us the leadership actions of listening to and following the instructions given to him that would lead to success. These are both critical leadership actions that we need to grasp in order to achieve success as leaders.

Listening is a critical aspect of leading successfully; and in all aspects of our leadership, we should be engaging with and listening to what God is telling us to do, trusting His message, and acting to carry out His commands. This is essential for many reasons. First of all, God cares about you and has a perfect plan for your life, including your career. Additionally, God cares about all the people He has placed under your leadership, and His way is best for them as well. In all the decisions we make, we should be placing God at the forefront while praying to Him for direction.

Often, we will be given directions that we do not understand how or why we are to follow them. Sometimes we may question if what we are hearing or feeling is coming from God because in our view following through would lead to failure. Proverbs 3:5 tells us to trust God with everything we have while shunning what we may think is best (NLT). God has been here since before the beginning of time (which was created for man) and will remain throughout eternity. Additionally, He knows everything that has happened, is happening, and will happen in the future. Who better to place our trust in than the One who already knows it all and has actually planned it all out!? Just rely on God's promise from Jeremiah 29:11 that declares that our future in not left to chance, but designed by God for each of us; and that left to His will, these plans are all for our benefit and good (NLT).

In order to hear what God is telling us and to trust Him enough to take action and follow His commands, we need to have a relationship with Him. We need to take the time to talk WITH God on a daily basis, and to make the time to sit quietly and listen to what He is telling us. We also need to walk with Him daily and live the life He has called us to live.

Joshua 1:9 commands us to be strong and courageous; and not to be scared or dismayed because the Lord has promised to be with us in all we do (NLT). First of all, when Joshua and the Israelites were told this, they were also told that this promise was reliant on the people of Israel obeying God's commands. This is why our daily walk with God is so important. Secondly, God already has a plan for our lives, and He also knows what the future holds. He even knows the bad decisions we will make and knows how to turn those outcomes for good. Who better to trust than the One who is in control? We need to build our relationship with God, talk to Him daily, listen to what He says, then follow His commands. He will never break our trust

.

Study Prayer

Lord God. Thank You for creating me special and for a unique purpose. Please allow me to hear Your will for me and understand what You are speaking to me. As You direct me in my life, I ask that You would intensify my trust in You while giving me the courage and strength to follow through with what is best for my life. Holy Spirit, please allow my trust in You to spill over into those I lead and direct them to You. In Jesus' Holy Name, Amen.

Questions

- If God directed you to leave your home and family and travel to a new place that you knew nothing about, in fact, you didn't even know where the endpoint was, how would you respond? If you have gone through this type of situation, how did things work out?

- As leaders, how can/does your response to God's commands affect others?

- Has God ever directed you to act in a way that was opposite of what you thought was the right decision? How did you respond? What was the outcome? What do you think would be different if you had responded differently?

- What does it mean to you as a leader to know that you walk with the One who knows the future?

- How is your relationship and daily walk with God? What can you do to strengthen this relationship?

- Explain how you see God's plan for you playing out in your life.

Reflection

Take a moment to reflect on this study and how putting this topic into practice can help prepare you for Eternity.

Honesty

"So please tell them you are my sister. Then they will spare my life and treat me well because of their interest in you." (Genesis 12:13, NLT)

We learn in Genesis 12 that no matter how godly we may be, that we are all sinners, and our sins can implicate others bringing trouble on them. As Abram travelled through the land that God had promised to him and his descendants a famine struck the land. Abram continued his travels South into Egypt. Genesis 12:13 tells us that Abram asked his wife, Sarai, to tell the people of Egypt that she was his sister because he feared being killed in response to their desire to have her (NLT). Since the Egyptians were told that Sarai was Abram's sister, they took her to Pharaoh to take as a wife/concubine, and Pharaoh in kind treated Abram well.

Regardless of what Pharaoh knew, God sent plagues into Pharaoh's household because Sarai was Abram's wife. The worse part of the story is that Abram did not learn from his mistake, nor did he learn to trust God in the exact same situation played out in Genesis 20 between Abraham and Abimelech, King of Gerar. This should also give us a sense of relief as we make the same mistakes over and again.

As leaders, especially servant leaders, honesty plays a vital role in building trust with our teams, but also in doing our part to protect them. Proverbs 16:28 advises that agitators cause problems while useless blathering leads to divisions (NLT). This verse speaks to two verbal wrongs, one being a gossip; however, we will concentrate on the lying aspect. Lying spreads strife, it brings trouble, and as we saw with Abram, the consequences can extend even to those who are not a part of the lie, and may not even know about the lie. God has placed us in positions of responsibility to protect those we lead from negative outcomes associated with lies.

God expects us to lead our people in a righteous manner. Remember, more important than leading our teams in whatever method our team has been assembled for, God has brought the team together for us to lead them to Him. We are shepherds. In modelling God to those we lead, honesty is a vital component that must be upheld. Proverbs 12:22 informs us that God hates lies, but that He finds pleasure in those who are honest (NLT). Do you expect God to bless you and your team if you are acting abominably to Him? Honesty is the best policy, and God will bless honesty.

Study Prayer

Jesus, I thank You right now for the leadership role that You have placed me in, and for the people that You have enlisted under my care. Please help me to see just how critical honesty is in leading them in a way that honors You. Holy Spirit, please be with me in all the decisions that I make throughout the day as well as in all my dealings with others and help me to be up forth and honest in all my interactions. In Jesus' Name, Amen.

Questions

- Why do you think Abram/Abraham lied twice instead of trusting the same God who had led him thus far?

- Are there times in the past when you have lied (or been less than honest) and it negatively impacted those you lead?

- If you are dealing with an issue now where you have been less than honest, do you see the benefit in letting the truth come out?

- What about transparency? Are there justified times when being less than honest, or hiding something is appropriate?

- What do you do when those above you tell you not to be transparent about an issue that will affect those you lead?

- Does the fact that a man chosen by God due to his righteousness made the same mistake twice and God continued to use him give you comfort in your life? Explain.

Reflection

Take a moment to reflect on this study and how putting this topic into practice can help prepare you for Eternity.

Peacemaker

"Finally Abram said to Lot, 'Let's not allow this conflict to come between us or our herdsmen.'" (Genesis 13:8, NLT)

We learn in Genesis 13 that as Abram and his nephew Lot began to settle in the land that God had led them too, God blessed both men with wealth in livestock leading to arguments and strife breaking out between their herdsmen. Desiring peace, Abram proposed a split between the two, allowing Lot to decide what land he wanted to inhabit. Lot looked around and chose the lush land of the valley, and ended up settling by the city of Sodom. Abram settled in Hebron and thanked God for what he had been given.

Abram saw trouble arising and increasing then decided to take actions to quell those issues.

He could have dictated to Lot where he was going to reside, but probably foresaw more issues down the road if Lot were to struggle; so, thinking ahead, Abram allowed Lot to choose, thus locking him into his decision. By choosing the abundant land, Lot also chose the area where relationships would be built with evil societies. Abram, on the other hand, was blessed by God and continued to thrive in the land where he settled.

Now, as leaders we are called to make decisions and choices on a daily basis; however, as servant leaders we should strive to find opportunities when we can allow those we lead to make some decisions. This is a good practice for multiple reasons. For starters, this is practice for ourselves, personally, at staying clear of micro-managing. Additionally, allowing others to make decisions offers them occasions that provide training moments for these same individuals who will become leaders in the future. This practice is good all the way around.

On another note, looking for circumstances where those we lead are trusted with some authority to make decisions is an act of peacemaking. This builds trust between the parties, and in the end, allows those we lead to see the pressures involved with decision-making and living with the choices we make. At the same time, the decisions being made are still under our discretion where we can step in as the leader and provide guidance, or conduct a full stop, before harmful choices proceed.

While giving the Beatitudes, in Matthew 5:9 Jesus praises peacemakers and assures that they will be called children of God (NLT). Look for openings that offer you an ability to provide training in decision-making while also building peace and trust with your people.

Remember that we are endeavoring to become servant leaders. This involves teaching those we lead and allowing learning opportunities. It also encompasses protecting these individuals, and we do this by carefully choosing what decisions to delegate to others, then offering guidance to them during the decision-making process.

Think back to when we were learning to make these same decisions and how what our leaders and mentors did or did not do could have helped us learn and become more successful. Now put this into context with Matthew 7:12 where Jesus lays out the Golden Rule. In this He states that we need to treat others the way that we want to be treated; going on to express that this was in reality what the Old Testament Law was intended for originally (NLT). This is what we are called to do, to be servant leaders. Trainers. Peacemakers.

Study Prayer

Lord Jesus, thank You for Abram's example of being a peacemaker; and thank You for encouraging me to become a peacemaker by promising to call me a child of God. Holy Spirit, I pray that You will guide me daily in my interactions and enable me to continually be a peacemaker among my team, my peers, and anyone else that I might encounter. Thank You for your help in growing my peacemaking ability. In Your Name, Amen.

Questions

- Did Abram set Lot up for failure by allowing him to choose to live by the people of Sodom? Explain.

- Explain how allowing others to make decisions is an act of peacemaking.

- Explain how peace between a leader and those they lead is a benefit. Explain how conflict hampers success.

- Explain how training others to take part in the decision-making process leads to peace.

- Discuss a time when you stepped back and allowed someone you led to make an important decision. How did that work out? What could you do differently in the future to help develop those you lead in the art of decision-making?

- Explain how delegating some decision-making processes to others also trains a leader to avoid micro-managing.

Reflection

Take a moment to reflect on this study and how putting this topic into practice can help prepare you for Eternity.

Surrounded

"But the people of this area were extremely wicked and constantly sinned against the Lord." (Genesis 13:13, NLT)

We found in the last study that Abram and Lot's wealth had grown to a point where their flocks were competing for pasture lands and water, which led to the two men's herdsmen fighting in the fields. To settle the situation down, Abram proposed to Lot that they would go their separate ways, then offered Lot his choice of land. Seeing the flourishing lands of the Jordan Valley, he went in that direction and settled near the city of Sodom. This move placed Lot in the vicinity of wicked people who did not worship God; and these people, and the relationships he developed with these people, would be life-changing for Lot and his family.

In most circumstances in our life and careers we are involved with people that we have little to no choice in the matter. Other times we choose individuals, for one reason or another, who might not have our moral, ethical, or religious views. Regardless of our situations, the world around us presents us with people, all day long, who the Bible would classify as wicked.

1 Peter 5:8 reminds us to constantly be on the lookout because the Devil is our enemy, and he is always looking for ways to destroy us (NLT). Now, this is not to suggest that we need to live life looking for a devil under every rock; but instead, we need to be aware of the people around us. Additionally, whether we place them in our lives or they are placed there by others, we need to influence them positively more than they influence us negatively.

With that being said, why wouldn't we pray to God and trust Him to give us the people to lead that He has for us? We can obviously pray for current team members, but why not be actively praying for future members as well? We may not know who these people will be, but these individuals are no secret to God. We should be praying that God would prepare our team members to strive to be their best; to be good team members; and most importantly, for their spiritual lives.

It is always our first job to model a godly life to those we lead and strive to help bring them closer to God. We know that God will answer these prayers because in Isaiah 41:10 we are reminded that we are not to fear or be distressed because God is with us. He is our strength and our help, and He is the source of our successes (NLT). God is on our side. He cares about us and those we lead. He places people in our lives; so, when we feel surrounded, we are surrounded by God, and the people that He has placed in our lives have been placed there for a purpose.

Study Prayer

Lord, I want to thank You this week for the times in my life when I feel surrounded by foes. Whether these foes be peers, or others who either purposefully or unintentionally taking actions that counter where I am trying to lead, or members of my team who push back against my leadership, these times provide an opportunity for me to grow my trust in You. I pray, dear Lord, that as I face these trying times, that You will grow my leadership abilities and allow me to know when to push forward and when to relent. Help me to see that not everybody who surrounds me is a foe, and enable me to reach those who do intend to oppose me and develop partnerships. Please allow these opportunities to give me the chance to show You to all of these individuals. In Your Name I Pray, Amen.

Questions

- Lot placed himself near the wicked people of Sodom. Knowing the full story, did Lot impact them, or did they impact him?

- How did Lot's decision to live amongst the people of Sodom impact his and his family's lives?

- Some people say that we should not surround ourselves with "evil" people. Is this possible? If we were able to isolate ourselves from "ungodly" people, who would reach them for God?

- Have you ever committed to faithfully praying for those you lead? What about those you will lead in the future? If so, what was the outcome?

- Explain how you model God to those you lead.

- Think about the one person you lead who is the most difficult to work with. How can you break down those walls and lead them to success in their career(s) while guiding them towards God?

Reflection

Take a moment to reflect on this study and how putting this topic into practice can help prepare you for Eternity.

Waiting

"So Sarai, Abram's wife, took Hagar the Egyptian servant and gave her to Abram as a wife. (This happened ten years after Abram had settled in the land of Canaan.)"
(Genesis 16:3, NLT)

God had promised to make Abram into a great nation and had ensured that this heir would come from his own body to fulfill this vow. As time went by, Abram's wife Sarai became impatient with her inability to bear a child. To "resolve" this issue, Sarai took matters into her own hands and gave her Egyptian maid, Hagar, to Abram as an additional wife. Hagar conceived a child, Ishmael, but this child was not the plan that God had to bring about His chosen people, Israel. Ishmael also became a great nation who has been a thorn in the side of Israel throughout history; and all of this came about because Abram and Sarai did not wait for God to fulfill his promise, which did come to pass, in God's perfect time, when Isaac was born.

Understanding that God has placed us in our roles as leaders, we must know that He has a plan for us, those we lead, and the organizations that we represent. Most of us have heard that when we ask God for something the response we get can be a "yes" or a "no," but most often what we hear and experience is "wait." We need to learn to see the benefits of waiting.

First and foremost, God knows what the future brings, and waiting will only provide value down the road. Secondly, waiting allows opportunities to present themselves and to flourish. Lastly, the time that we spend waiting is a training period where God is molding us in preparation for what He has for us in the future. Lamentations 3:25 advises us that God is good to those who wait on Him, and that during this time of waiting we should be inquiring of Him (NLT).

Another word for God would be faithful, but our willingness to wait is critical to His faithfulness coming to fruition, and this time spent waiting is best devoted to building our relationship with God and seeking Him. Additionally, we need to learn to separate the act of waiting from a routine of procrastination.

Waiting is not fun. Oftentimes it feels stressful, burdensome, and/or even tiring. We are reassured in Isaiah 40:31 that, "[But] those who trust in the Lord will find new strength. They will soar high on wings like eagles. They will run and not grow weary. They will walk and not faint" (NLT). When we wait for God's perfect timing and for Him to move all the pieces into place, He will open the right door at the right time. During this waiting period, He will give us peace as we draw closer to Him, and the end result will be exactly what He has for us, which will be perfect.

Always remember, however, it is our requirement of having a relationship with God to continually seek Him; otherwise, when we make decisions and try to force the changes we think God has for us, we will not see God's perfect plan for us and things will end up being harder for us and those around us.

Study Prayer

Heavenly Father. One of the Fruits of the Spirit is Patience. Sometimes I struggle with this, and I want to ask forgiveness for the times that I try to rush things. Please teach me patience, and allow me to learn and grow in my times of waiting. Help me to know when You're saying "Yes," "No," or "Wait." Thank You for growing me in my times of waiting. In Jesus' Name, Amen.

Questions

- How has Abram's act to conceive Ishmael with Hagar impacted the people of Israel throughout history?

- Who was at fault in the decision, Sarai or Abram? Why?

- Do you have a close enough relationship with God to have an idea what He has planned for your life?

- What plan do you believe God is working out for you? What do you believe God is trying to teach you during your waiting time?

- In your current situation, how do you separate waiting from procrastination?

- Explain how God comforts you and gives you peace during your waiting periods.

- How can acting on your own effect you, those you lead, and your organization?

Reflection

Take a moment to reflect on this study and how putting this topic into practice can help prepare you for Eternity.

Putting It All Together

Leadership in Eternity: It's All About the Heart

"Don't you realize that someday we believers will judge the world? And since you are going to judge the world, can't you decide even these little things among yourself? Don't you realize that we will judge angels? So you should surely be able to resolve ordinary disputes in this life." (1 Corinthians 6:2-3, NLT)

The purpose of this book series is to layout Biblical ideals of leadership hidden throughout the book of Genesis. In particular, this book covers Genesis 1-16, and the overlaying topic revolves around *Training for More*. In other words, we are learning about God's desire for us to use our leadership roles here on Earth to prepare ourselves for Eternity.

Oh, the interesting thoughts and ideas that ran through each of our minds when this topic was first introduced. Think back. Was being open-minded easy as we journeyed further on through the studies? Well, let's consider this topic a little more, as this will continue to be an important topic to consider in future books.

Our scripture for this week's study lays out rather clearly that we will have very high-level responsibilities in God's Eternal Kingdom. Let's be real! "Judging the world" and "judging angels" is not a minor calling. This makes our current roles seem so small and petty; however, our time here on this earth is our proving ground. This is where we prove to God that we are good stewards with the responsibilities that He has given to us.

Our motivating factor in becoming leaders in the mold of Jesus should be Matthew 25:23. We should all be striving to hear the words, "Well done, my good and faithful servant. You have been faithful in handling this small amount, so now I will give you many more responsibilities. Let's celebrate together!" (NLT). The NSA version ends with "Enter into the joy of your Master." Hearing those words from our Savior, and spending Eternity in His presence will make anything we have dealt with on this earth worth our struggles.

We have studied many topics in this book, and there will be many more subjects in books to come, and growing our skills in these areas will enable us to become more godly leaders here on earth; although the issues we face in this life will not be the same as those that will be present in Heaven. Afterall, Revelation 21:4 assures us that earthly issues will die along with this earth and we will not face death, loss, or pain anymore (NLT). The struggles of this earth will be no more. Heaven will be a place of peace, so the leadership issues that we have studied here will be no more.

Instead, this God ordained growth in leadership is more about the heart. In Matthew 20:26-28 Jesus reminds us that because He has chosen us, we are not like the rest of the world. Our difference would be shown in our actions towards others. We are to lower ourselves and act as servants of others. To be as a slave, just as Jesus was during His time on this earth, then proved through His death to save us all (NLT).

We are called to live out His story to those we lead, but as humans, this requires a heart change. Revelation 21:27 shows how important this heart change is by reminding us that, "Nothing evil will be allowed to enter, nor anyone who practices shameful idolatry and dishonesty—but only those whose names are written in the Lamb's Book of Life" (NLT). It's all about the heart!

So, our responsibilities here on earth is to spend our time as leaders preparing our hearts for service in God's Eternal Kingdom. Daniel 7:27 encourages us that all kingdoms and dominions under Heaven will be handed over to us as Children of God, and that we will lead these entities in serving and obeying Jesus (NLT). Only the pure heart of a servant leader is capable of this leadership.

Finally, Isaiah 9:7 assures us that Jesus' Kingdom of Peace will continue to expand and will have no end. It continues by saying that through God, righteousness and justice will reign forever (NLT). We're striving to be apart of this Kingdom. All we have to do to be a leader in this glorious eternity is allow God to create His heart inside of us through our leadership calling. Are you willing and ready to prepare to take part in this *Training for More*?

Study Prayer

Jesus, Thank You again for calling me to be a leader. Thank You for each of the individuals that You have placed under my care. Holy Spirit, please work within me to help me become a better leader; and most importantly, please help me to use my leadership to represent You to those I lead. Please allow me to think beyond the world that I live in and begin to understand and comprehend the eternal Kingdom that I am preparing for here on Earth. Create in me a clean heart, Your heart, and use me and train me to complete the goals that You have for me in Your Kingdom. Amen!

Questions

- What was your initial thoughts about training for a role in Eternity? Were you able to proceed with an open-mind? What are your thoughts now?

- What do you think about what 1 Corinthians 6:2-3 says about "judging the world" and "judging angels?" Explain how you think this plays out. Discuss how this changes your thinking about Eternity.

- Discuss how the lessons in this book lend themselves to creating a pure heart designed for a servant leader.

- Think about how you see leadership in Heaven playing out, then put pen to paper and describe your thoughts.

- Explain how allowing God to affect and change your heart can lead to you being a better example to those you lead. How can you live out Jesus' story in front of those you lead?

- Are you willing and able to prepare to take part in *Training for More*? To what extent?

Reflection

Take a moment to reflect on everything we have studied and how putting what we have learned into practice can help prepare you for Eternity.

Bibliography

All Biblical translations are New Living Translation unless specifically identified otherwise.

Holy Bible, New Living Translation. Carol Stream, IL: Tyndale House Publishers, 2015.

New American Standard Bible. La Habra, CA: The Lockman Foundation, 1993.

Made in the USA
Coppell, TX
18 June 2026

81942774R00075